Halal Wealth Strategies

Build Ethical Wealth in Islam
Hussain Hydrose

Halal Wealth Strategies

Chapters 1
Introduction 3
The Foundations of Islamic Finance 7
Halal Investment Strategies for Muslims 12
Shariah-Compliant Financial Products 18
Islamic Finance for Beginners 23
Zakat and Wealth Management in Islam 29
Ethical Investing in Islam 35
Riba-Free Finance Options 41
Islamic Debt Management Tips 47
Building Long-Term Wealth with Integrity 53
Case Studies of Successful Muslim Investors 58
Conclusion: A Path to Ethical Wealth 62

1.
2.
3.
4.
5.
6.
7.
8.
9.
10.
11.
12.

Chapters

- **Introduction to Halal Wealth** : What is halal wealth? Why is it important for Muslims to grow wealth ethically? Set the stage for the book, outlining the key principles.

- **The Foundations of Islamic Finance** : Explain key concepts such as *riba* (interest), *gharar* (excessive uncertainty), and the ethical principles of Islamic finance.

- **Halal Investment Strategies for Muslims** : Offer actionable strategies and highlight permissible investment opportunities, such as real estate, Shariah-compliant stocks, and mutual funds.

- **Shariah-Compliant Financial Products** : Dive into specific financial tools and products that adhere to Islamic law, including *Murabaha* (cost-plus financing) and *Ijara* (leasing).

- **Islamic Finance for Beginners** : Break down the basics of Islamic financial principles for those just starting, including key terms, basic investment principles, and budgeting tips.

- **Zakat and Wealth Management in Islam** : Explore the critical role of *Zakat* in wealth management, how to calculate it, and its spiritual and social benefits.

- **Ethical Investing in Islam** : Discuss how Muslims can invest in businesses that align with Islamic values, such as ethical technology or sustainable agriculture.

- **Riba-Free Finance Options** : Outline alternatives to conventional banking and interest-based loans, including Islamic banks and Shariah-compliant financing options.

- **Islamic Debt Management Tips** : Provide practical advice for managing debt in accordance with Islamic values, including strategies for avoiding excessive debt and interest.

- **Building Long-Term Wealth with Integrity** : Summarize how Muslims can ensure that their wealth-building efforts are sustainable, ethical, and aligned with Islamic values.

- **Case Studies of Successful Muslim Investors** (Optional): Offer real-world examples of Muslims who have successfully navigated the world of Islamic finance.

- **Conclusion: A Path to Ethical Wealth** : Recap the book's key takeaways, emphasizing the importance of wealth management in Islam and the benefits of adhering to ethical principles.

Introduction

Introduction to Halal Wealth

What is Halal Wealth?

Halal wealth refers to money, assets, or property that is acquired, managed, and utilized in accordance with Islamic law (Shariah). The term "halal" means permissible, indicating that wealth must be obtained in ways that are ethically, morally, and legally compliant with Islamic teachings. This means avoiding earnings that come from prohibited activities (*haram*), such as interest-based financial transactions (*riba*), gambling (*maysir*), or investments in industries that are contrary to Islamic principles, such as alcohol, pork, or other unethical businesses.

In Islam, wealth is not just a measure of financial success but a test from Allah, intended to be used responsibly and for the betterment of oneself, family, and society. Halal wealth is an essential part of a Muslim's faith, as it directly influences one's standing before Allah in both this world and the Hereafter.

Why is it Important for Muslims to Grow Wealth Ethically?

1. **Wealth as a Trust from Allah**

    In Islam, wealth is viewed as an **amanah** (trust) from Allah. It is not inherently good or bad, but the way in which it is earned, managed, and spent defines its ethical status. Muslims are instructed to view their wealth as a blessing and a test from Allah, ensuring that they manage it in a way that reflects their obedience to Him. Ethical wealth management is seen as a way to gain Allah's pleasure and earn reward in both this life and the Hereafter. **Key Verse:** "And know that your wealth and your children are but a trial and that Allah has with Him a great reward." (Surah Al-Anfal 8:28) This verse illustrates that wealth, while a blessing, is also a test. It comes with responsibilities, and Muslims must ensure that their financial activities align with the ethical guidelines laid out in the Quran and the Sunnah.

2. **Avoiding Haram Earnings**

Halal wealth is directly tied to avoiding haram earnings. Islam strictly prohibits earning money through unethical or harmful means. This includes activities like gambling, usury (interest), or investing in industries that promote harm to society, such as alcohol or weapons production. By adhering to halal methods of wealth generation, Muslims can ensure that their financial activities do not compromise their faith. **Key Verse:** "O you who have believed, do not consume interest, doubled and multiplied, but fear Allah that you may be successful." (Surah Al-Imran 3:130) This verse forbids *riba* (interest), one of the most significant prohibitions in Islamic finance. Interest-based transactions exploit the borrower and create economic disparity, which is why Islam encourages alternative financial models based on fairness and shared risk.

3. **Social Responsibility and Justice**

Islam emphasizes the importance of social responsibility when it comes to wealth. Wealth should be used not just for personal benefit but to uplift the community and contribute to societal well-being. The concept of *Zakat* , the obligatory charity, ensures that wealth is redistributed to support the needy, thus reducing inequality. Growing wealth ethically involves making sure that earnings are clean and that a portion of them is used to support the less fortunate. **Key Verse:** "Take from their wealth a charity by which you purify them and cause them increase, and invoke [Allah's blessings] upon them." (Surah At-Tawbah 9:103) Zakat purifies wealth and ensures its ethical distribution, demonstrating that ethical wealth-building in Islam goes beyond personal gain—it is also about contributing to social justice and economic equality.

4. **Long-Term Sustainability and Integrity**

One of the key principles of halal wealth-building is sustainability. Islam encourages Muslims to focus on long-term financial growth rather than short-term gains, which often come through unethical or high-risk methods. Halal wealth is rooted in stability, fairness, and integrity. Investments and business dealings should be transparent and based on mutual benefit, with no exploitation or unfair advantage taken by one party over another. **Hadith Reference:** The Prophet Muhammad (PBUH) said: *"The best earnings are those of a man's own hand, and from every business transaction which is considered halal." (Sunan Ibn Majah)* This Hadith encourages Muslims to earn wealth through hard work and permissible transactions, highlighting the importance of personal integrity in wealth accumulation.

Key Principles of Halal Wealth

1. **Prohibition of Riba (Interest)**
   Interest (*riba*) is strictly forbidden in Islamic finance because it is considered exploitative and unjust. In Islamic economics, transactions must involve shared risk and reward, meaning that both parties in a financial deal benefit fairly from the outcome.

2. **Avoiding Gharar (Uncertainty and Speculation)**
   Transactions that involve excessive risk or uncertainty (*gharar*) are prohibited in Islamic finance. This includes speculative investments or gambling-like activities where outcomes are unpredictable and can lead to significant financial loss. Instead, Islamic finance promotes transparency and informed decision-making in all business dealings.

3. **Permissible Business Ventures**
   Muslims are encouraged to engage in business ventures that are halal and beneficial to society. This includes industries like healthcare, education, and ethical

businesses that do not violate Islamic laws. Halal investments focus on ethical business practices that contribute positively to both society and the environment.

4. **Zakat and Charity**

Wealth in Islam is seen as incomplete if it is not shared with those in need. Zakat, one of the Five Pillars of Islam, is an obligation for Muslims to give a portion of their wealth to the poor and needy. By doing so, wealth is purified and its blessings are increased.

Setting the Stage for the Book

Throughout this book, we will explore how Muslims can grow wealth ethically by adhering to Islamic financial principles. Each chapter will break down different aspects of halal wealth-building, from investment strategies to managing debt in a riba-free way. The goal is to equip you with practical tools to navigate the complexities of modern finance while staying true to Islamic teachings. Whether you're an entrepreneur, investor, or someone looking to manage your personal finances, this book will provide you with actionable insights for building wealth that is both halal and sustainable.

As you embark on this journey, remember that wealth in Islam is not just a sign of success but a means to fulfill your obligations to Allah and society. By following the principles laid out in this book, you will not only grow your financial resources but also ensure that your wealth serves as a source of blessing for you and those around you.

In the upcoming chapters, we will dive deeper into specific areas such as halal investments, ethical business practices, managing Zakat, and avoiding riba, helping you build a strong foundation for long-term financial success in alignment with your faith.

The Foundations of Islamic Finance

The Foundations of Islamic Finance

Islamic finance offers a comprehensive ethical framework that is rooted in the Quran and Sunnah, prioritizing fairness, transparency, and social welfare. Unlike conventional financial systems, which often emphasize profit maximization, Islamic finance is based on principles that promote justice and equity for all parties involved. This chapter will explore three core concepts central to Islamic finance: **riba** (interest), **gharar** (excessive uncertainty), and the overarching ethical principles that govern financial transactions.

---

1. Riba (Interest)

One of the most well-known prohibitions in Islamic finance is **riba**, which refers to any form of interest or usury. Riba occurs when a lender charges an additional amount beyond the principal sum, often without the borrower receiving any added benefit in return. The Quran explicitly forbids riba, as it is viewed as exploitative and unjust.

Key Verse: "O you who have believed, do not consume interest, doubled and multiplied, but fear Allah that you may be successful." (Surah Al-Imran 3:130)

Riba is considered haram (forbidden) because it leads to wealth concentration in the hands of a few, exacerbating social inequality and economic disparity. By earning money through interest, lenders profit without sharing the risks associated with the transaction, while the borrower bears the full burden. This one-sided dynamic violates the ethical tenets of fairness and justice that Islam upholds.

Islamic finance seeks to eliminate this inequality by promoting **profit-and-loss sharing models**, such as **Mudarabah** (profit-sharing partnerships) and **Musharakah** (joint ventures). In these models, all parties involved share the risks and rewards equitably, ensuring that no one party benefits disproportionately at the expense of another.

Example of Prohibited Riba :

- In a conventional loan, a bank lends $10,000 and charges 10% interest. The borrower must repay $11,000 regardless of whether they benefit from the loan. This would be considered riba in Islamic finance because the lender profits without sharing any risk or effort.

Islamic Alternative :

- In a **Murabaha** transaction (cost-plus financing), a bank purchases a commodity and resells it to the buyer for a profit. The buyer knows the original cost and the profit margin upfront, ensuring transparency and mutual consent.

---

2. Gharar (Excessive Uncertainty)

The concept of **gharar** refers to uncertainty, ambiguity, or risk in contractual agreements. Islamic finance prohibits any transaction that involves excessive uncertainty, as it can lead to exploitation or unfairness. In essence, **gharar** means that all parties involved in a contract must have a clear understanding of the terms and the outcome of the transaction.

Key Verse: *"O you who have believed, do not consume one another's wealth unjustly or send it [in bribery] to the rulers in order that [they might aid] you [to] consume a portion of the wealth of the people in sin, while you know [it is wrong]."* (Surah Al-Baqarah 2:188)

This verse speaks to the ethical requirement that wealth must be obtained through just and transparent means. Gharar is prohibited because it introduces ambiguity, which could lead to one party gaining unfairly at the expense of another. For example, gambling and speculative financial products (such as derivatives) often involve high levels of uncertainty, where the outcome is unknown and risks are disproportionately borne by one party.

Examples of Prohibited Gharar :

- **Short-selling** : Involves selling assets not yet owned with the hope of buying them at a lower price later. The future outcome is uncertain and speculative, making this form of trading haram.
- **Derivatives Trading** : Includes contracts like options or futures, where the value depends on the future price of an asset. This speculative nature introduces significant uncertainty.

Islamic Alternative :

- In Islamic finance, contracts like **Istisna** (where the price and quality of goods are agreed upon before manufacturing begins) and **Salam** (advance purchase of goods) are used to ensure clarity, fairness, and predictability.

---

3. Ethical Principles of Islamic Finance

Islamic finance operates on a foundation of ethical principles designed to promote justice, equity, and social responsibility. These principles ensure that financial transactions benefit all parties involved and contribute to the broader welfare of society. The key ethical principles are:

1. **Prohibition of Haram Activities** : Islamic finance prohibits investments or business dealings that involve activities deemed haram in Islam, such as gambling, alcohol production, and businesses related to pork. This ensures that wealth is generated through permissible and ethical means.

2. **Transparency and Honesty in Transactions** : Contracts and agreements in Islamic finance must be clear, transparent, and free from deception or dishonesty. Both parties must fully understand the terms and conditions, ensuring that neither party is misled or exploited. **Hadith Reference** : The Prophet Muhammad (PBUH) said:

"The seller and the buyer have the right to keep or return goods as long as they have not parted, and if they spoke the truth and made clear the defects, then they would be blessed in their bargain." (Sahih al-Bukhari) This Hadith emphasizes the importance of truthfulness and transparency in trade, ensuring that both parties are fully informed about the product and its conditions.

3. **Wealth Distribution through Zakat** :
One of the Five Pillars of Islam, *Zakat* ensures that wealth is redistributed to benefit the less fortunate. Zakat purifies wealth and ensures that the economic system is balanced by supporting those in need. Islamic finance emphasizes the importance of contributing to societal welfare through charitable giving, making wealth-building a community-oriented endeavor.

4. **Profit-and-Loss Sharing** :
Unlike conventional finance, which focuses on fixed interest returns, Islamic finance encourages profit-and-loss sharing. This ensures that all parties share the risks and rewards of any venture. Financial models like **Mudarabah** (where one party provides capital and the other expertise) and **Musharakah** (joint ventures) are built on this principle, promoting cooperation and fairness.

Summary

Islamic finance is more than just a system of managing money—it is a framework for promoting ethical behavior, fairness, and social responsibility. The prohibition of **riba** ensures that wealth is not accumulated through exploitation, while the ban on **gharar** guarantees that financial transactions are transparent and fair. These principles, alongside an emphasis on ethical business practices and wealth redistribution through **Zakat** , create a holistic system that aligns financial success with moral and spiritual fulfillment.

By adhering to the foundations of Islamic finance, Muslims can grow their wealth in a way that benefits not only themselves but also their community and the broader society. The upcoming chapters will dive deeper into how to apply these principles practically, guiding you on how to build wealth while upholding your religious and ethical responsibilities.

Halal Investment Strategies for Muslims

Halal Investment Strategies for Muslims

As Muslims, growing wealth ethically and in accordance with Islamic principles is essential. The concept of halal investments is central to Islamic finance, emphasizing that wealth should be accumulated in a way that benefits both the individual and society while staying within the boundaries of Shariah (Islamic law). Halal investments avoid activities considered haram, such as *riba* (interest), *gharar* (excessive uncertainty), and industries like alcohol, gambling, and pork production. Instead, they focus on permissible ventures that promote fairness, transparency, and shared benefit.

This chapter offers actionable halal investment strategies and highlights specific opportunities for Muslims looking to grow their wealth in a Shariah-compliant manner. Some of the most popular avenues include **real estate**, **Shariah-compliant stocks**, and **halal mutual funds**.

---

1. Real Estate Investment

Real estate is one of the most favored halal investment opportunities in Islamic finance due to its tangible and enduring nature. Properties provide a source of rental income, which is considered halal as long as it does not involve prohibited activities, and offer long-term growth potential through property appreciation.

Why Real Estate is Halal:

- It involves tangible assets, reducing the uncertainty or speculation (*gharar*) that is forbidden in Islamic finance.
- Rental income, when generated from permissible activities, is halal.
- Investors share the risks and rewards through rental income or property appreciation.

Types of Real Estate Investments:

- **Rental Properties** : Buying residential or commercial property to rent out is a straightforward way to earn halal income. As long as the rental agreement is clear, fair, and free from interest-based lending, this can be an excellent source of steady income.

- **Real Estate Development** : Engaging in property development is another halal opportunity. It involves building homes or commercial spaces for sale or lease, offering both growth and the satisfaction of contributing to community infrastructure.

Actionable Tips for Real Estate Investment :

1. **Research the Local Market** : Before investing in real estate, it's essential to research the property market in your area to ensure the property has potential for rental income or appreciation.

2. **Focus on Ethical Tenants** : Ensure your rental properties are leased to businesses or individuals engaged in halal activities.

3. **Explore Shariah-Compliant Mortgages** : Many Islamic financial institutions offer halal mortgage products that allow Muslims to buy properties without engaging in interest-based loans. These often involve *Murabaha* (cost-plus financing) or *Ijara* (leasing).

---

2. Shariah-Compliant Stocks

Shariah-compliant stocks are shares in companies that adhere to Islamic guidelines. Investing in these stocks allows Muslims to participate in equity markets without compromising their values. However, not all companies listed on stock exchanges are halal, so it's essential to invest only in businesses that meet Islamic criteria.

Criteria for Shariah-Compliant Stocks :

1. **Business Activity** : The company's primary business activities must be halal. For example, companies involved in alcohol, gambling, interest-based financial services, or pork products are strictly prohibited.
2. **Debt Levels** : Companies with high levels of interest-based debt may not be Shariah-compliant, even if their core activities are permissible.
3. **Earnings from Prohibited Sources** : Companies earning significant income from prohibited sources (such as interest or haram products) are not halal.

How to Find Shariah-Compliant Stocks :

- **Shariah Screening Tools** : Many financial institutions offer Shariah-compliant screening tools that help identify halal stocks. Popular Shariah indices include the **Dow Jones Islamic Market Index (DJIM)** and **FTSE Shariah Global Equity Index Series** .
- **Islamic Stock Screening Apps** : Apps like **Zoya** or **Islamicly** provide users with real-time information on whether a stock is halal or haram.

Actionable Tips for Stock Investment :

1. **Use Shariah-Compliant Brokers** : Seek out brokers or platforms that specialize in Shariah-compliant investments. Some platforms will automatically screen out non-compliant companies.
2. **Diversify Your Portfolio** : Like any other investment, it's essential to diversify your portfolio to mitigate risk. Focus on various industries such as technology, healthcare, and ethical consumer goods.
3. **Purification of Wealth** : Sometimes, a small portion of earnings from Shariah-compliant stocks may come from non-halal sources (e.g., interest income). In this case, Islamic investors are encouraged to purify their income by donating that portion to charity.

3. Halal Mutual Funds

Halal mutual funds pool investors' money to invest in Shariah-compliant stocks, bonds, and other assets. These funds are managed by professionals who ensure that all investments align with Islamic principles. For many Muslims, mutual funds offer an easy way to diversify their portfolio without needing to manually screen each investment for compliance with Islamic law.

Benefits of Halal Mutual Funds :

- **Diversification** : Investing in a broad range of stocks and assets minimizes risk while increasing the potential for returns.
- **Professional Management** : Halal mutual funds are managed by experienced professionals who handle compliance with Shariah, making it easier for individual investors to invest without constantly monitoring each stock.
- **Transparency** : These funds often publish detailed reports on their holdings and the steps taken to ensure Shariah compliance.

Popular Halal Mutual Funds :

- **Amana Mutual Funds Trust** : One of the most popular halal mutual fund families, offering growth and income funds that strictly adhere to Islamic principles.
- **Wahed Invest** : A robo-advisor that provides access to halal investment portfolios, including Shariah-compliant stocks, sukuk (Islamic bonds), and real estate.

Actionable Tips for Investing in Halal Mutual Funds :

1. **Research Fund Managers** : Ensure that the mutual fund manager or institution is knowledgeable in Shariah-compliant finance.
2. **Check Historical Performance** : Look at the fund's performance over time to gauge its stability and growth potential.

3. **Consider Expense Ratios** : While halal mutual funds are an excellent option for hands-off investors, pay attention to management fees and expense ratios to avoid eroding your profits.

---

4. Sukuk (Islamic Bonds)

Sukuk , often referred to as Islamic bonds, offer a halal alternative to conventional interest-bearing bonds. Sukuk represent ownership in a tangible asset or project rather than a debt obligation. Investors in sukuk receive returns generated by the asset, such as rent from real estate or profits from a business venture.

Why Sukuk Are Halal :

- Sukuk do not involve interest payments; instead, returns are based on the actual performance of the asset.
- The underlying asset in a sukuk must be halal, ensuring compliance with Islamic law.

Actionable Tips for Sukuk Investment :

1. **Research Available Sukuk Offerings** : Sukuk are often issued by governments or large corporations. Look for stable issuers and halal projects.
2. **Understand the Risk Profile** : As with any investment, sukuk carries risks. Ensure you understand the asset's potential for returns and risks before investing.

Conclusion: A Balanced Halal Portfolio

By incorporating a mix of real estate, Shariah-compliant stocks, halal mutual funds, and sukuk into your portfolio, you can build wealth in a manner that is both ethical and aligned with your faith. The key is to seek long-term stability, ethical transparency, and investments that contribute positively to society.

Islamic finance provides Muslims with a range of halal investment opportunities, ensuring that they can grow their wealth while adhering to the ethical guidelines laid out by the Quran and Sunnah. With these strategies, you can ensure that your financial growth is both spiritually rewarding and financially successful.

Shariah-Compliant Financial Products

Shariah-Compliant Financial Products

Shariah-compliant financial products are designed to help Muslims engage in financial transactions while adhering to Islamic principles. These products avoid activities that are explicitly prohibited in Islamic law, such as earning interest (*riba*), engaging in excessive uncertainty (*gharar*), or investing in unethical industries. Instead, Islamic financial products emphasize transparency, fairness, and shared risk, ensuring that all parties benefit equitably from the transaction. This chapter will dive into two of the most popular Shariah-compliant financial products: **Murabaha** (cost-plus financing) and **Ijara** (leasing).

---

1. Murabaha (Cost-Plus Financing)

Murabaha is one of the most widely used Shariah-compliant financial products, particularly in home financing and business transactions. In a Murabaha agreement, the Islamic financial institution buys a product or asset (such as a home, car, or equipment) on behalf of the customer and then sells it back to the customer at a marked-up price. This price includes the original cost plus an agreed-upon profit margin. Importantly, the price is fixed, and both the buyer and the financial institution are aware of the profit margin from the start.

Murabaha differs from a conventional loan because it does not involve interest charges on the loaned amount. Instead, it is a sale contract where the financial institution earns a profit for facilitating the transaction.

How Murabaha Works :

1. The customer identifies the asset they wish to purchase (e.g., a home).

2. The Islamic bank or financial institution purchases the asset on behalf of the customer.
3. The bank then sells the asset to the customer at a pre-agreed price that includes the original cost plus a profit margin.
4. The customer repays the bank in installments or in full, depending on the terms of the agreement.

Example of Murabaha in Practice : Imagine a customer wants to buy a house for $200,000 but does not have the full amount upfront. The bank purchases the house for $200,000 and sells it to the customer for $220,000, agreeing that the customer can repay this amount over the next 10 years in equal monthly installments. Both parties know the total amount due upfront, and no additional interest or fees will be charged.

Key Benefits :

- **Transparency** : The profit margin and final price are agreed upon at the beginning, ensuring that there are no hidden fees or interest charges.
- **Compliance with Shariah Law** : Murabaha avoids *riba* (interest) by structuring the transaction as a sale rather than a loan.
- **Flexibility** : Murabaha can be used in various transactions, including home financing, vehicle purchases, and even business equipment acquisition.

Actionable Tips for Murabaha :

1. **Choose a Reputable Islamic Bank** : Make sure the bank or financial institution you are dealing with follows Shariah-compliant procedures to ensure the transaction is valid.
2. **Negotiate Terms** : While the profit margin is fixed, you can negotiate the installment plan, which may affect the total repayment time.

2. Ijara (Leasing)

Ijara, which means "to rent" or "to lease" in Arabic, is another Shariah-compliant financial product that is widely used, especially in property, equipment, and vehicle financing. In an Ijara agreement, the financial institution purchases an asset and leases it to the customer. The customer then makes lease payments to the financial institution for the use of the asset over a specified period. At the end of the lease term, the customer may have the option to purchase the asset or simply return it.

Ijara works similarly to a conventional leasing arrangement, but without the involvement of interest. Instead, the payments made by the customer are based on the rental or lease of the asset, which remains in the ownership of the financial institution until the lease term is complete.

How Ijara Works :

1. The customer identifies an asset (e.g., a vehicle or a piece of machinery) they wish to lease.
2. The Islamic bank purchases the asset on behalf of the customer.
3. The customer leases the asset from the bank, making regular lease payments.
4. At the end of the lease term, the customer may have the option to purchase the asset at a predetermined price or return it to the bank.

Example of Ijara in Practice : A business wants to lease a piece of equipment to operate its factory. The bank purchases the equipment for $100,000 and leases it to the business for $2,000 per month for five years. The business uses the equipment and makes lease payments. At the end of five years, the business can either buy the equipment for a nominal amount (as per the agreement) or return it to the bank.

Key Benefits :

- **No Ownership Risk for Customer** : Since the bank retains ownership of the asset during the lease term, the customer is not responsible for any ownership risks (such as depreciation).

- **Flexibility** : Ijara is suitable for financing various assets, from cars to homes and business equipment.
- **Option to Own** : At the end of the lease term, customers often have the option to purchase the asset, making Ijara similar to rent-to-own arrangements.

Actionable Tips for Ijara :

1. **Understand the Terms** : Make sure the lease payments, asset ownership details, and final purchase price (if applicable) are clearly laid out before entering into the agreement.
2. **Asset Maintenance** : In some Ijara contracts, the responsibility for maintaining the asset may fall on the customer. Clarify the responsibilities for maintenance and repairs in the lease agreement.

Other Popular Shariah-Compliant Financial Products

While Murabaha and Ijara are two of the most widely used Shariah-compliant financial tools, there are several other products that are worth considering:

1. **Mudarabah (Profit-Sharing Agreement)** :
   In a Mudarabah agreement, one party provides the capital, while the other provides the expertise to manage the investment. Profits are shared between the parties according to a pre-agreed ratio, but losses are borne solely by the capital provider. This structure ensures that both parties share the risks and rewards equitably.

2. **Musharakah (Joint Venture)** :
   Musharakah is a joint partnership where two or more parties contribute capital to a business or investment. Profits are shared based on the agreed ratio, while losses are shared according to the capital contribution of each partner. Musharakah is commonly used in business partnerships and real estate financing.

3. **Sukuk (Islamic Bonds)** :
   Sukuk represents ownership in a tangible asset or project, rather than a debt

obligation. Sukuk holders receive returns generated by the asset, such as rent from a property or profits from a business venture. Sukuk is an excellent Shariah-compliant alternative to conventional bonds, offering fixed returns without involving interest.

Conclusion: Ethical Financial Tools for Muslim Investors

Shariah-compliant financial products like **Murabaha** and **Ijara** offer Muslims a way to engage in financing and investment while adhering to Islamic principles. These tools ensure transparency, fairness, and shared risk, making them ideal for ethical wealth-building. Whether you're looking to purchase a home, lease a vehicle, or finance your business, Islamic financial products provide a viable and halal alternative to conventional loans and leasing models.

By using these products, Muslims can grow their wealth, finance large purchases, and invest in their future without compromising their faith.

Islamic Finance for Beginners

Islamic Finance for Beginners

Islamic finance offers an alternative to conventional financial systems by adhering to the principles laid out in Islamic law, or **Shariah** . Its primary focus is on promoting ethical financial practices, avoiding interest (riba), and ensuring fairness and transparency in all transactions. For those just starting, this chapter will break down the basic principles of Islamic finance, define key terms, and provide actionable budgeting and investment tips to help you manage your finances in line with Islamic teachings.

---

1. Key Principles of Islamic Finance

Islamic finance is based on several foundational principles that distinguish it from conventional financial systems. Understanding these principles is essential for beginners:

1. **Prohibition of Riba (Interest)** :
   - One of the fundamental tenets of Islamic finance is the absolute prohibition of interest, known as **riba** . Interest-based transactions are considered exploitative because they allow one party to benefit without sharing risk. In Islamic finance, risk-sharing and profit-sharing are emphasized, which ensures fairness in transactions.
   - **Key Verse:**
     "O you who have believed, do not consume interest, doubled and multiplied, but fear Allah that you may be successful." (Surah Al-Imran 3:130)

2. **Avoidance of Gharar (Excessive Uncertainty)** :

- Islamic finance prohibits transactions that involve excessive uncertainty or speculation, known as **gharar**. This principle ensures that all parties involved in a transaction have clear and transparent information, reducing the likelihood of exploitation.
- **Example:** Gambling or speculative investments like derivatives are prohibited because of their uncertainty and high risk.

3. **Profit-and-Loss Sharing (PLS)** :
   - Islamic finance promotes shared risk and reward through models like **Mudarabah** (profit-sharing) and **Musharakah** (joint ventures). These agreements ensure that all parties contribute to and benefit from the outcome of a business or investment. If there is a profit, it is shared based on pre-agreed terms; if there is a loss, it is also shared proportionately.

4. **Zakat (Obligatory Charity)** :
   - **Zakat** is one of the Five Pillars of Islam and a critical component of Islamic finance. It requires Muslims to give 2.5% of their wealth to the needy, helping to redistribute wealth in society and reduce inequality.

5. **Ethical Investments** :
   - Investments in industries that are harmful or considered unethical, such as alcohol, gambling, or pork, are strictly prohibited. Islamic finance encourages investment in businesses that promote social good and are in line with Shariah principles.

2. Key Terms in Islamic Finance

For those new to Islamic finance, understanding key terms is essential. Below are some of the most common terms used in Islamic finance:

1. **Halal** : Permissible according to Islamic law.

- Example: Halal investments refer to financial activities and products that comply with Shariah law.
2. **Riba** : Interest or usury, prohibited in all forms.
    - **Example:** Charging interest on a loan is considered riba and is not allowed in Islamic finance.
3. **Mudarabah** : A profit-sharing partnership where one party provides capital, and the other provides expertise.
    - **Example:** In a Mudarabah agreement, profits are shared based on pre-agreed terms, but the financial loss is borne only by the investor.
4. **Musharakah** : A joint venture where all parties contribute capital and share both profits and losses.
    - **Example:** Musharakah is used in property investments, where multiple partners share ownership and income from rental properties.
5. **Ijara** : Leasing or renting. This is used for financing assets like cars, homes, or equipment. The financial institution owns the asset and leases it to the customer for a fixed term.
    - **Example:** A customer leases a vehicle from a bank, making monthly payments, and may purchase the vehicle at the end of the lease term.
6. **Sukuk** : Islamic bonds that represent ownership in a tangible asset or project, providing returns to the investor.
    - **Example:** Governments and corporations issue Sukuk to raise funds for projects like real estate development or infrastructure.
7. **Takaful** : Islamic insurance, where participants pool resources to protect against financial loss, distributing risk among all participants.
    - **Example:** Takaful insurance is based on mutual cooperation, with profits and losses shared by policyholders.

3. Basic Investment Principles in Islamic Finance

As a beginner, understanding how to invest in accordance with Islamic finance is key to growing your wealth while staying true to your faith. Here are some basic principles to guide you:

1. **Avoid Interest-Based Investments** :
   - As interest is prohibited in Islamic finance, avoid conventional bonds, savings accounts, or any investment vehicle that involves interest payments. Instead, look for **halal investment options** , such as **Sukuk** (Islamic bonds) or **Shariah-compliant mutual funds** .

2. **Invest in Ethical and Halal Industries** :
   - Always ensure that your investments are in industries that are permissible under Shariah law. For example, healthcare, technology, and real estate are generally considered halal sectors, while gambling, alcohol, and tobacco are prohibited.

3. **Consider Real Estate** :
   - Real estate is often seen as a safe and halal investment option. It provides a tangible asset, which aligns with Islamic principles of reducing uncertainty and risk. Rental income generated from property is considered halal as long as the property is used for permissible purposes.

4. **Profit-Sharing Investments** :
   - Look for investment opportunities that involve profit-sharing or equity participation, such as **Mudarabah** or **Musharakah** . These models ensure fairness and align with Islamic principles by distributing profits and losses equitably.

4. Budgeting Tips for Beginners in Islamic Finance

Effective budgeting is a crucial part of managing personal finances in accordance with Islamic principles. Here are some basic tips to get you started:

1. **Track Your Income and Expenses** :
   - Create a monthly budget that tracks your income and expenditures. This will help you avoid overspending and ensure you are living within your means, as encouraged by Islamic teachings.
   - **Tip** : Use budgeting apps or a simple spreadsheet to categorize your spending into essentials (e.g., housing, groceries) and non-essentials.

2. **Allocate for Zakat** :
   - Set aside 2.5% of your annual savings and earnings to fulfill your **Zakat** obligation. This is not only a religious duty but also a way to purify your wealth and contribute to the well-being of society.
   - **Tip** : Set up an automated savings plan or use a Zakat calculator to ensure you meet your obligations.

3. **Save for Long-Term Goals** :
   - Islam encourages financial prudence and planning for the future. Allocate a portion of your income towards long-term goals like buying a home, saving for retirement, or investing in education.
   - **Tip** : Consider halal savings plans, such as **Shariah-compliant pensions** or **Takaful savings plans** , which allow you to save and grow your wealth without compromising your faith.

4. **Avoid Debt Whenever Possible** :
   - While debt is not entirely prohibited, Islamic finance discourages excessive debt, especially if it involves interest. If you must take on debt, seek out halal alternatives such as **Murabaha** (cost-plus financing) or **Ijara** (leasing).

- **Tip** : Focus on building an emergency fund to cover unexpected expenses and avoid relying on loans.

Conclusion: Starting Your Journey in Islamic Finance

As a beginner in Islamic finance, it is important to start by understanding the core principles that guide ethical financial behavior. By avoiding interest, investing in halal industries, and prioritizing fairness and transparency in transactions, you can grow your wealth in a way that is aligned with your faith. Whether you are budgeting for your daily expenses or planning for long-term investments, Islamic finance offers you the tools and principles to ensure that your financial success is both spiritually and materially rewarding.

This chapter lays the foundation for more advanced topics, such as halal investment strategies and Shariah-compliant financial products, which will be explored in greater detail in the following chapters.

Zakat and Wealth Management in Islam

Zakat and Wealth Management in Islam

Zakat is one of the Five Pillars of Islam and serves as a foundational aspect of wealth management for Muslims. It is a mandatory act of charity, deeply rooted in the belief that wealth is a trust from Allah and must be used for the benefit of society, particularly the less fortunate. Zakat not only helps to purify wealth but also plays a crucial role in reducing inequality, promoting social justice, and supporting the welfare of the Muslim community. This chapter explores the critical role of Zakat in Islamic wealth management, how to calculate it, and the profound spiritual and social benefits it offers.

---

1. The Importance of Zakat in Islam

In Islam, Zakat is viewed as an obligation, not merely a charitable contribution. Its primary goal is to redistribute wealth and ensure that the most vulnerable members of society are supported. The word "Zakat" comes from the Arabic root meaning "to purify" or "to grow," symbolizing the purification of one's wealth and soul by giving a portion to those in need.

Key Verse: *"Take from their wealth a charity by which you purify them and cause them increase, and invoke [Allah's blessings] upon them."* (Surah At-Tawbah 9:103)

This verse emphasizes that Zakat not only purifies wealth but also brings blessings and growth to the giver. By contributing to the welfare of the less fortunate, Muslims ensure that their wealth is ethical and in line with the moral and spiritual teachings of Islam.

Zakat as a Pillar of Wealth Management

In terms of wealth management, Zakat serves several key purposes:

- **Redistribution of Wealth** : Zakat helps reduce economic disparity by redistributing a portion of the wealth from those who have more to those who are in need.

- **Encouragement of Savings** : Zakat is due only on savings that have been held for a year (above the nisab, or minimum threshold), encouraging Muslims to save and manage their wealth responsibly.

- **Wealth Purification** : By paying Zakat, Muslims purify their wealth from greed and selfishness, fostering a sense of community and responsibility.

2. How to Calculate Zakat

Calculating Zakat is a straightforward process, but it requires careful consideration of one's assets and liabilities. Zakat is due on certain types of wealth, and the amount is typically 2.5% of the total assets that have been held for at least one lunar year.

Zakatable Assets

Zakat is due on the following types of assets:

- **Cash and Savings** : Any cash on hand, in bank accounts, or held in the form of savings must be considered for Zakat.

- **Gold and Silver** : Jewelry made of gold or silver, as well as bullion, is Zakatable. Other precious metals or stones are exempt unless they are used for investment.

- **Stocks and Investments** : Profits from investments or Shariah-compliant stocks that are held for at least one lunar year are subject to Zakat.

- **Business Assets** : For business owners, Zakat is calculated on inventory, receivables, and profits, while liabilities and expenses are deducted.

Non-Zakatable Assets

Zakat is not due on the following assets:

- **Primary Residence**: The home in which you live is exempt from Zakat, as it is considered a necessity.
- **Personal Items**: Items like clothing, furniture, and appliances are not subject to Zakat.
- **Debts Owed to You**: If someone owes you money and is unable to repay it, this debt is temporarily exempt from Zakat until it is repaid.

Nisab (Minimum Threshold)

To be eligible to pay Zakat, one's wealth must exceed the **nisab**, which is the minimum amount of wealth a Muslim must have before Zakat becomes obligatory. The nisab is equivalent to:

- **85 grams of gold**, or
- **595 grams of silver**

Since the market value of gold and silver fluctuates, it is essential to calculate the nisab based on current prices.

Zakat Formula

Once you determine your Zakatable assets, calculating Zakat is as simple as applying the following formula:

$$\text{Zakat} = \frac{2.5}{100} \times \text{Zakatable Assets}$$

For example, if a person has $10,000 in Zakatable assets, the Zakat due would be:

$$\text{Zakat} = \frac{2.5}{100} \times 10,000 = 250$$

Thus, the individual would pay $250 in Zakat for the year.

3. The Spiritual Benefits of Zakat

Zakat is not merely a financial obligation; it carries profound spiritual significance for Muslims. Paying Zakat is a means of purifying one's soul and wealth. Here are some key spiritual benefits of Zakat:

- **Purification of Wealth and Soul** : Zakat cleanses wealth from the impurities of greed and selfishness. It also purifies the soul by fostering humility and gratitude.
  Hadith Reference : The Prophet Muhammad (PBUH) said: *"Charity does not decrease wealth."* *(Sahih Muslim)* This Hadith highlights the spiritual belief that giving in charity leads to blessings and an increase in one's wealth, both materially and spiritually.
- **Strengthening Ties with the Community** : Zakat fosters a sense of solidarity and compassion within the Muslim community. By supporting those in need, the giver develops a stronger bond with the community and ensures that wealth circulates in a way that benefits everyone.
- **Gratitude and Contentment** : Paying Zakat reminds the wealthy of their blessings, fostering gratitude and a sense of responsibility. It helps reduce attachment to material possessions and cultivates contentment in life.

4. The Social Benefits of Zakat

In addition to its spiritual benefits, Zakat plays a vital role in the social and economic well-being of the Muslim community. By redistributing wealth, Zakat ensures that society's most vulnerable are cared for and that economic disparities are minimized.

Reducing Poverty and Inequality

One of the primary objectives of Zakat is to alleviate poverty. Zakat funds are distributed to those who are most in need, including:

- **The Poor (Al-Fuqara')** : Those who lack sufficient means to meet their basic needs.
- **The Needy (Al-Masakeen)** : Individuals who may have some means but are still struggling to meet their daily expenses.
- **Debtors (Al-Gharimin)** : Individuals burdened by debt that they are unable to repay.

By supporting these groups, Zakat reduces poverty, narrows the wealth gap, and ensures that wealth circulates more equitably.

Promoting Social Welfare

Zakat is used not only for direct financial assistance but also for initiatives that promote long-term social welfare. This can include building schools, hospitals, and other essential infrastructure that benefits society as a whole.

Preventing Hoarding of Wealth

Islam discourages the hoarding of wealth, as it leads to economic stagnation and social inequality. Zakat serves as a tool to prevent wealth from being accumulated in the hands of a few, ensuring that it continues to circulate and benefit society.

Key Verse: *"And those who hoard gold and silver and spend it not in the way of Allah, give them tidings of a painful punishment." (Surah At-Tawbah 9:34)*

This verse warns against hoarding wealth and emphasizes the importance of using it in ways that benefit others.

Conclusion: Zakat as a Tool for Ethical Wealth Management

Zakat is a cornerstone of Islamic wealth management, offering both spiritual rewards and social benefits. By calculating and paying Zakat, Muslims fulfill a crucial religious obligation while contributing to the economic well-being of their community. It purifies wealth, reduces poverty, promotes social welfare, and prevents the hoarding of resources. In doing so, Zakat ensures that wealth is used as a tool for good, rather than as a source of greed or exploitation.

Through Zakat, Muslims not only manage their wealth ethically but also earn Allah's blessings and increase their standing in both this world and the Hereafter.

Ethical Investing in Islam

Ethical Investing in Islam

In Islam, investing is not just about growing wealth—it's about growing wealth *ethically* . Ethical investing in Islam refers to making financial decisions that align with Shariah (Islamic law), which emphasizes fairness, justice, and social responsibility. This approach ensures that all investments not only generate returns but also contribute to the greater good, avoiding industries or practices that are harmful to individuals and society. In this chapter, we will explore how Muslims can invest in businesses that align with Islamic values, such as ethical technology, sustainable agriculture, and other sectors that contribute positively to the world.

1. Core Principles of Ethical Investing in Islam

Ethical investing in Islam is governed by several key principles derived from the Quran and Sunnah:

- **Avoidance of Haram (Prohibited Activities)** : Muslims are prohibited from investing in industries that engage in haram activities, such as alcohol production, gambling, pork, and interest-based financial services. This is because these industries are harmful to individuals and society, violating the ethical guidelines set by Islam.

- **Promoting Social Good** : Ethical investing means supporting industries and businesses that align with Islamic values by promoting social welfare, environmental sustainability, and the well-being of communities. Islam encourages Muslims to engage in productive activities that benefit humanity as a whole.

- **Ensuring Fairness and Transparency** : Investments should be made in a manner that is free from exploitation, fraud, and excessive uncertainty (*gharar*). Islamic finance prioritizes transparency and fairness in transactions, ensuring that both parties in a financial arrangement share the risks and rewards equitably.

- **Profit-and-Loss Sharing** :
  Islam promotes the sharing of both profits and risks in business ventures through models such as **Mudarabah** (profit-sharing partnerships) and **Musharakah** (joint ventures). This encourages ethical business practices and ensures that wealth is not accumulated unjustly.

2. Ethical Investment Opportunities for Muslims

There are several ethical sectors where Muslims can invest in accordance with Islamic principles. Below, we will discuss some of the most prominent ethical industries, focusing on how they align with Islamic values.

A. Ethical Technology

Technology is one of the fastest-growing industries globally and offers numerous opportunities for ethical investing. Ethical technology companies focus on using innovation to improve society, whether through renewable energy, healthcare solutions, or improving access to education.

Key Sectors in Ethical Technology :

- **Renewable Energy** :
  Companies that develop and promote solar, wind, and other renewable energy technologies are considered halal investment opportunities. These companies help reduce the reliance on fossil fuels and combat climate change, aligning with the Islamic principle of environmental stewardship. **Example** : Investing in a company that produces solar panels or wind turbines can be considered halal because it contributes to sustainable development and reduces harm to the environment.

- **Healthcare Technology** :
  Innovations in healthcare, such as medical devices, telemedicine, and biotech solutions, align with the Islamic value of promoting health and well-being. These companies aim to improve the quality of life for individuals, making them an ethical investment option for Muslims. **Example** : Investing in companies that develop life-saving medical technologies, such as cancer treatments or telemedicine platforms, can be considered ethical as they contribute to human welfare.

B. Sustainable Agriculture

Sustainable agriculture is another sector that aligns with Islamic values, particularly in terms of environmental responsibility and food security. Investing in businesses that prioritize organic farming, responsible water use, and sustainable land management can be a halal way to grow wealth while contributing to global food security.

Key Aspects of Sustainable Agriculture :

- **Organic Farming** :
  Companies that focus on organic farming avoid the use of harmful chemicals and genetically modified organisms (GMOs). This practice ensures that food production is healthier for consumers and more sustainable for the environment. **Example** : Investing in an organic farming company that promotes pesticide-free, sustainable agriculture can be considered halal, as it minimizes harm to both people and the environment.

- **Water Conservation** :
  Islam teaches the importance of conserving natural resources, especially water. Investing in companies that develop water-efficient irrigation systems or promote sustainable water usage in farming aligns with Islamic principles. **Example** : Supporting a business that develops irrigation technologies to conserve water in drought-prone regions is not only environmentally responsible but also aligns with the Islamic value of preserving natural resources.

C. Socially Responsible Investments (SRI)

Socially responsible investments (SRI) are those that focus on ethical, sustainable, and socially conscious business practices. These investments avoid industries involved in environmental degradation, unethical labor practices, and human rights violations. SRIs often focus on companies that prioritize fair trade, environmental sustainability, and social justice.

Key Considerations for SRI :

- **Fair Trade Practices** : Companies that follow fair trade practices ensure that workers in developing countries receive fair wages and work in safe conditions. This aligns with the Islamic principle of justice and the prohibition of exploitation. **Example** : Investing in a company that ensures fair wages and ethical working conditions in its supply chain can be considered halal, as it promotes social justice and human dignity.

- **Environmental Stewardship** : Businesses that prioritize environmental sustainability, such as those involved in carbon-neutral initiatives or reforestation projects, are aligned with Islamic values that encourage environmental conservation. **Example** : Investing in a company that works to reduce carbon emissions or replant forests can be viewed as halal, as it contributes to protecting the environment for future generations.

3. Shariah-Compliant Investment Platforms and Tools

To help Muslims invest ethically, several platforms and financial tools have been developed that screen companies and investments for Shariah compliance. These platforms help investors ensure that their financial activities are aligned with Islamic principles.

Shariah-Compliant Mutual Funds and ETFs :

- **Amana Mutual Funds** :
  This fund family screens investments to ensure they align with Islamic principles, avoiding industries like alcohol, gambling, and interest-based financial services. Amana's funds are widely recognized and offer ethical investment opportunities in sectors like healthcare and technology.

- **Wahed Invest** :
  Wahed Invest is a robo-advisor that provides access to a diversified portfolio of Shariah-compliant investments. The platform offers a range of halal investment options, including ethical stocks and Sukuk (Islamic bonds), making it easier for Muslims to invest according to their values.

Shariah Stock Screening Tools :

- **Zoya** :
  Zoya is a popular app that helps users screen stocks for Shariah compliance. The app provides real-time information on whether a stock is halal or haram, helping Muslims make informed investment decisions.

- **Islamicly** :
  Islamicly is another screening tool that provides detailed insights into Shariah-compliant stocks. It ranks companies based on their adherence to Islamic principles, helping users avoid haram investments.

---

4. Actionable Steps for Ethical Investing

For Muslims interested in ethical investing, here are some practical steps to get started:

1. **Research Shariah-Compliant Platforms** :
   Use halal investment platforms like Wahed Invest or Amana Mutual Funds to access pre-screened, Shariah-compliant investments.

2. **Screen Companies for Shariah Compliance**:
Use tools like Zoya or Islamicly to ensure that the companies you are investing in comply with Islamic principles. These tools can help you avoid industries that are not aligned with your values.

3. **Diversify Your Investments**:
Ethical investing doesn't mean putting all your money into one sector. Diversify your portfolio by investing in a mix of sectors, such as ethical technology, sustainable agriculture, and socially responsible companies.

4. **Monitor Your Investments**:
Regularly review your investments to ensure that they remain Shariah-compliant and continue to align with your ethical goals. If a company no longer meets these criteria, consider divesting.

Conclusion: Growing Wealth with Purpose

Ethical investing in Islam is about more than just financial returns—it's about ensuring that your investments contribute to the well-being of society and align with Islamic values. By investing in sectors like ethical technology, sustainable agriculture, and socially responsible businesses, Muslims can grow their wealth while promoting justice, environmental stewardship, and human dignity.

Shariah-compliant tools and platforms make it easier than ever for Muslims to engage in ethical investing, allowing you to grow your wealth in a manner that is both halal and socially conscious. Ultimately, ethical investing is about using wealth as a force for good, ensuring that financial success aligns with both spiritual and moral principles.

Riba-Free Finance Options

Riba-Free Finance Options

Islam strictly prohibits *riba* (interest) in all financial transactions, as it is considered exploitative and unjust. In contrast to conventional banking, where interest-based loans and savings accounts are the norm, Islamic finance provides several alternatives that comply with Shariah principles. These **riba-free finance options** ensure that Muslims can engage in financial activities without compromising their faith. In this chapter, we will explore various Shariah-compliant alternatives to conventional banking and loans, including **Islamic banks** and specific financing products like **Murabaha**, **Ijara**, and **Mudarabah**.

---

1. The Prohibition of Riba in Islamic Finance

The Quran unequivocally prohibits *riba* (interest), as it leads to economic injustice and exploitation. Interest-based transactions allow one party to profit without sharing the risk, often at the expense of the borrower, who is burdened with paying more than the principal amount.

Key Verse :
"O you who have believed, do not consume interest, doubled and multiplied, but fear Allah that you may be successful." (Surah Al-Imran 3:130)

By eliminating interest, Islamic finance promotes fairness, shared risk, and mutual benefit. This ensures that all financial transactions are ethical and aligned with the values of justice and equity.

---

2. Islamic Banking: A Riba-Free Alternative

Islamic banks operate under the principles of Shariah, offering riba-free financial products and services. These banks do not charge interest or engage in interest-based lending. Instead, they use profit-sharing models and asset-backed financing to facilitate financial transactions in a manner that aligns with Islamic law.

Key Features of Islamic Banking :

- **No Interest** : Islamic banks do not charge or pay interest on loans, savings, or deposits. Instead, they provide alternative models like profit-sharing and leasing.
- **Asset-Backed Financing** : Transactions are based on tangible assets, ensuring that both the lender and the borrower share the risks and rewards.
- **Ethical Investments** : Islamic banks avoid investing in industries that are considered haram (prohibited), such as alcohol, gambling, or tobacco.

Popular Islamic Banks :

- **Al Rajhi Bank** (Saudi Arabia): One of the largest Islamic banks in the world, offering a range of riba-free financial services, including home and car financing, savings accounts, and business loans.
- **Dubai Islamic Bank** (UAE): A pioneer in Islamic banking, offering Shariah-compliant mortgages, investment accounts, and personal loans.

How to Choose an Islamic Bank :

1. **Research Shariah Compliance** : Ensure that the bank adheres to Shariah principles and offers riba-free products.
2. **Check Available Services** : Look for services that meet your financial needs, whether it's for personal financing, business loans, or investment opportunities.

3. Riba-Free Financing Options

Several Islamic financing products have been developed to offer alternatives to conventional interest-based loans. These products include **Murabaha** (cost-plus financing), **Ijara** (leasing), **Mudarabah** (profit-sharing), and **Musharakah** (joint ventures). Each of these products allows Muslims to finance their needs without engaging in riba.

A. Murabaha (Cost-Plus Financing)

Murabaha is one of the most widely used Shariah-compliant financing methods. It is often used in home financing, vehicle loans, and business transactions. In a Murabaha contract, the financial institution purchases an asset on behalf of the customer and sells it back to them at a profit. This profit margin is agreed upon upfront, and the customer repays the total amount in installments.

How Murabaha Works :

1. The customer identifies the asset they wish to purchase (e.g., a house or a car).
2. The Islamic bank buys the asset on behalf of the customer.
3. The bank sells the asset to the customer at a predetermined price, which includes the bank's profit margin.
4. The customer repays the bank in fixed installments over a set period.

Example :

A customer wishes to purchase a home for $200,000. The bank buys the property and sells it to the customer for $220,000, with the additional $20,000 being the bank's profit. The customer pays this amount back over 10 years in fixed monthly installments.

B. Ijara (Leasing)

Ijara is a leasing contract in which the financial institution buys an asset and leases it to the customer for a fixed period. The customer makes regular lease payments to the bank.

At the end of the lease term, the customer may have the option to purchase the asset for a nominal amount.

How Ijara Works :

1. The bank buys the asset (e.g., a vehicle or property) and leases it to the customer.
2. The customer makes regular payments to the bank, which are treated as rent for using the asset.
3. At the end of the lease period, the customer can either purchase the asset or return it to the bank.

Example :

A customer leases a car from an Islamic bank for $500 per month for five years. At the end of the lease, the customer may choose to purchase the car for a nominal fee.

Benefits of Ijara :

- No interest payments, as the payments are treated as rent.
- The customer does not own the asset until the lease term is complete, reducing ownership risks.

C. Mudarabah (Profit-Sharing)

Mudarabah is a profit-sharing partnership where one party provides the capital, and the other provides expertise or management. Profits are shared according to a pre-agreed ratio, but any losses are borne solely by the capital provider.

How Mudarabah Works :

1. One party (the investor) provides the capital, and the other (the entrepreneur) manages the investment.
2. Profits are shared based on the agreed ratio.
3. If there is a loss, it is borne solely by the investor, while the entrepreneur loses only their time and effort.

Example :

An investor provides $50,000 to an entrepreneur to start a business. They agree to split the profits 70% (investor) and 30% (entrepreneur). If the business succeeds and makes $10,000 in profit, the investor gets $7,000, and the entrepreneur gets $3,000.

Benefits of Mudarabah :

- Risk-sharing between the investor and the entrepreneur.
- Encourages entrepreneurship and business development within a Shariah-compliant framework.

D. Musharakah (Joint Venture)

Musharakah is a joint partnership where all parties contribute capital and share both the profits and losses based on their capital contribution. It is commonly used in real estate financing and business ventures.

How Musharakah Works :

1. Two or more parties contribute capital to a project or investment.
2. Profits are shared based on the agreed ratio, while losses are shared in proportion to each party's capital contribution.
3. All parties have a say in the management of the project or investment.

Example :

Two partners contribute $100,000 each to start a real estate project. They agree to share profits and losses equally. If the project generates $20,000 in profit, each partner receives $10,000. If there is a loss, both partners share the loss equally.

Benefits of Musharakah :

- Encourages cooperation and shared responsibility in business ventures.
- Aligns with Islamic principles of fairness and risk-sharing.

4. Islamic Microfinance

Islamic microfinance provides small, riba-free loans to individuals and small businesses who may not have access to conventional financing. These loans often use models like Murabaha or Qard Hasan (benevolent loans) to help individuals start or expand businesses, improve their living conditions, or access essential services like education and healthcare.

Example :

An Islamic microfinance institution may provide a $500 interest-free loan to a small business owner to purchase equipment. The business owner repays the loan in small, manageable installments over time, without incurring interest.

Conclusion: Riba-Free Finance for a Just Economy

Riba-free finance options offer Muslims ethical alternatives to conventional banking and interest-based loans. By using products like **Murabaha** , **Ijara** , **Mudarabah** , and **Musharakah** , individuals can finance homes, cars, and businesses while remaining true to Islamic principles. Islamic banks and microfinance institutions play a crucial role in offering these Shariah-compliant solutions, ensuring that Muslims can grow their wealth and fulfill their financial needs without engaging in prohibited activities. By choosing riba-free finance options, Muslims contribute to a just and equitable economic system that benefits both individuals and society as a whole.

Islamic Debt Management Tips

Islamic Debt Management Tips

Debt is a part of many people's lives, but in Islam, managing debt responsibly is critical. Islamic principles emphasize the importance of avoiding excessive debt, not engaging in interest-bearing transactions (*riba*), and repaying debts promptly. This chapter provides practical advice for managing debt in accordance with Islamic values, offering strategies to avoid falling into overwhelming debt and interest-based loans.

---

1. Avoid Interest-Based Debt

Islam strictly prohibits *riba* (interest), which is considered exploitative and unjust. Taking on debt that incurs interest can lead to a cycle of financial hardship, where the borrower is continuously burdened with additional payments. Avoiding interest-based debt is a core principle in Islamic finance.

Key Verse :
"O you who have believed, fear Allah and give up what remains [due to you] of interest, if you should be believers." (Surah Al-Baqarah 2:278)

Strategies to Avoid Interest-Based Debt :

- **Seek Islamic Financing** : Look for Shariah-compliant financial products, such as **Murabaha** (cost-plus financing) or **Ijara** (leasing), which allow you to borrow money or finance large purchases without engaging in interest.
- **Use Interest-Free Credit Cards** : Some financial institutions offer halal credit cards that operate on a fee-based model instead of charging interest on outstanding balances.

- **Negotiate Payment Plans**: If you're facing a situation where you might have to incur debt, negotiate an interest-free installment plan with the lender, especially in cases involving large purchases like home or car financing.

2. Prioritize Repaying Debt

In Islam, paying off debts promptly is considered an ethical obligation. The Prophet Muhammad (PBUH) emphasized the importance of clearing debts, and delaying repayment without a valid reason is discouraged. Prolonged indebtedness can lead to financial instability and emotional stress.

Hadith Reference: The Prophet Muhammad (PBUH) said: "The soul of a believer is held hostage by his debt until it is paid off." (Sunan Ibn Majah)

Tips for Prioritizing Debt Repayment:

- **Create a Debt Repayment Plan**: Make a clear plan to pay off your debts as soon as possible. Prioritize high-interest or haram debt first, then focus on clearing the remaining amounts.
- **Budget for Debt Repayment**: Allocate a specific portion of your monthly budget to debt repayment. This will help you keep track of your payments and avoid falling behind.
- **Avoid Delaying Payments**: Delaying debt repayments without a valid reason is discouraged in Islam. If you're struggling to make payments, communicate with your lender to seek an extension or installment plan that works for both parties.

3. Avoid Excessive Debt

Islam encourages financial prudence, and taking on excessive debt for non-essential purposes is discouraged. Debt should only be incurred when necessary, such as for basic needs, education, or business investments, and even then, it should be kept to a minimum.

Key Verse :
"And those who, when they spend, are neither extravagant nor miserly, but choose a moderate way between the two."
(Surah Al-Furqan 25:67)

Strategies to Avoid Excessive Debt :

- **Live Within Your Means** : Avoid unnecessary spending and luxury purchases that can lead to taking on more debt. Prioritize essential needs like housing, food, and education before considering additional expenses.

- **Build an Emergency Fund** : Having an emergency fund can help you cover unexpected expenses without resorting to loans. Aim to save at least 3-6 months' worth of living expenses to handle emergencies.

- **Avoid Credit Cards for Non-Essentials** : Credit cards can be a major source of debt if used irresponsibly. Limit credit card use to essential or planned purchases, and avoid using them for discretionary spending.

4. Seek Islamic Debt Management Solutions

If you're already in debt, it's important to seek halal methods to manage and repay it. Several Islamic financial tools can help Muslims handle debt in ways that align with their faith.

A. Qard Hasan (Benevolent Loans)

Qard Hasan refers to an interest-free loan provided to someone in need, with the expectation that it will be repaid without any additional charges. This type of loan is an ideal alternative to conventional interest-bearing loans.

How Qard Hasan Works :

- The lender provides a loan without expecting any financial benefit or interest.
- The borrower agrees to repay the loan according to the agreed-upon timeline.

If you're struggling with debt, seek help from family, friends, or community members who might be willing to offer a Qard Hasan loan to help you pay off your obligations.

B. Islamic Debt Consolidation Plans

Some Islamic financial institutions offer debt consolidation services, where they pay off multiple debts and restructure the payment plan into a single, interest-free arrangement. This simplifies repayment and can help borrowers avoid riba and late fees.

Example :

An Islamic bank may offer a Murabaha-based debt consolidation plan, where they purchase your debt from different lenders and allow you to repay them through structured installments without incurring interest.

---

5. Practice Financial Discipline and Avoid Unnecessary Loans

One of the keys to avoiding debt is practicing financial discipline. Islam encourages moderation in all aspects of life, including spending. By carefully managing your finances and making thoughtful decisions, you can avoid the need for loans and live within your means.

Hadith Reference :

The Prophet Muhammad (PBUH) said:

"The best of you are those who are best in paying off their debts."
(Sahih al-Bukhari)

Practical Tips for Financial Discipline :

- **Create and Stick to a Budget** : A well-structured budget helps track income and expenses, making it easier to avoid debt. Include categories for essential expenses, savings, and debt repayment.

- **Save Before You Spend** : Save for large purchases instead of relying on loans or credit cards. This not only helps avoid debt but also teaches financial patience and discipline.

- **Avoid Impulse Purchases** : Impulsive buying can quickly lead to debt. Always ask yourself if a purchase is necessary and whether you can afford it without borrowing.

6. Negotiate Debt Repayment if Necessary

In cases where you are unable to repay your debts due to financial hardship, Islam encourages compassion and leniency. If you're struggling to make payments, speak to your lender about renegotiating the terms or extending the repayment period.

Key Verse :

"And if someone is in hardship, then [let there be] postponement until [a time of] ease. But if you give [from your right as] charity, then it is better for you."
(Surah Al-Baqarah 2:280)

Steps to Renegotiate Debt :

- **Communicate with Your Lender** : Be proactive in discussing your financial difficulties with your lender. Most lenders are willing to renegotiate terms to avoid defaults.

- **Request a Payment Extension** : If you need more time to repay, ask for an extension or installment plan that reduces the monthly payment amount.

- **Seek Forgiveness or Reduction** : In some cases, especially with Islamic lenders, you may be able to negotiate a partial forgiveness of the debt or a reduction in the principal amount.

7. Make Dua for Debt Relief

Islam encourages Muslims to seek help from Allah in all matters, including financial difficulties. Making **dua** (supplication) for debt relief is an important spiritual practice that brings peace of mind and comfort during challenging times.

Dua for Debt Relief :
"O Allah, suffice me with what is lawful and keep me away from what is unlawful, and by Your grace, make me independent of all others." (Sunan al-Tirmidhi)

Reciting this dua regularly can bring spiritual relief and encourage you to make ethical financial decisions.

Conclusion: Managing Debt with Integrity

Debt management in Islam is about more than just paying off obligations—it's about maintaining financial integrity, avoiding interest, and practicing responsibility. By following Islamic principles, such as avoiding excessive debt, prioritizing debt repayment, and using Shariah-compliant financing options, Muslims can manage their financial affairs ethically and in accordance with their faith. With careful planning, discipline, and reliance on Allah, Muslims can navigate debt responsibly while protecting their financial well-being and spiritual growth.

Building Long-Term Wealth with Integrity

Building Long-Term Wealth with Integrity

Building wealth in Islam is not simply about accumulating financial assets; it's about ensuring that the methods used to generate, manage, and distribute wealth are aligned with Islamic values. Islamic teachings emphasize that wealth is a blessing from Allah, and it must be earned and spent in ways that are ethical, sustainable, and beneficial to both the individual and society. This chapter will summarize how Muslims can ensure that their wealth-building efforts are in harmony with their faith, focusing on sustainability, ethics, and integrity.

1. Wealth as a Trust from Allah

In Islam, wealth is seen as a **trust** (*amanah*) from Allah, and it must be handled with care and responsibility. Muslims are taught that wealth should be earned through halal (permissible) means and used in ways that are beneficial not only to the individual but also to the community at large.

Key Verse :
"And know that your wealth and your children are but a trial and that Allah has with Him a great reward."
(Surah Al-Anfal 8:28)

This verse reminds Muslims that wealth is a test from Allah. The way in which it is accumulated and used reflects one's faith and ethical standing. It is important to view wealth as a tool for fulfilling both personal and societal obligations, rather than as an end in itself.

2. Ethical Wealth Accumulation

Wealth must be accumulated through **halal** means. This includes engaging in business or employment that adheres to Islamic guidelines, avoiding prohibited industries such as alcohol, gambling, or pork, and steering clear of any practices that exploit others.

Key Principle: Avoiding Riba (Interest)
One of the core prohibitions in Islamic finance is *riba* (interest). Muslims are required to avoid interest-bearing loans and investments, as *riba* leads to unfair economic disparity and exploitation.

Key Strategy: Halal Investments
Muslims are encouraged to invest in businesses and industries that align with Islamic values, such as ethical technology, healthcare, and sustainable agriculture. By investing in Shariah-compliant sectors, Muslims ensure that their wealth is not only halal but also contributes positively to the well-being of society.

Hadith Reference:
The Prophet Muhammad (PBUH) said: *"The best earnings are those of a man's own hand, and from every business transaction which is considered halal."* (Sunan Ibn Majah)

---

3. Sustainable Wealth Management

Sustainability is a key aspect of wealth management in Islam. Wealth should not be hoarded or spent recklessly; instead, it should be managed in a way that ensures long-term financial stability and contributes to the betterment of society.

Key Principle: Moderation in Spending
Islam encourages **moderation** in spending, advising Muslims to avoid extravagance while also avoiding stinginess. Balanced spending ensures that wealth is used effectively without leading to wastefulness.

Key Verse:

"And those who, when they spend, are neither extravagant nor miserly, but choose a moderate way between the two." (Surah Al-Furqan 25:67)

Key Strategy: Zakat and Charity

One of the ways to ensure sustainable wealth is by giving **Zakat** (obligatory charity) and **Sadaqah** (voluntary charity). Zakat purifies wealth and redistributes it to those in need, helping to reduce inequality and poverty within the community.

Key Verse:

"Take from their wealth a charity by which you purify them and cause them increase, and invoke [Allah's blessings] upon them." (Surah At-Tawbah 9:103)

Zakat not only benefits the recipient but also ensures the spiritual purification of the giver's wealth, making it a central pillar of ethical wealth management in Islam.

4. Long-Term Investment Strategies

Muslims are encouraged to adopt **long-term investment strategies** that promote steady and sustainable growth. This avoids the speculative and high-risk behavior that Islam prohibits under the concept of *gharar* (excessive uncertainty). Long-term investments in real estate, Shariah-compliant stocks, or halal mutual funds are seen as prudent ways to grow wealth in a sustainable manner.

Key Strategy: Ethical Real Estate Investment

Real estate is a popular and halal form of long-term investment. It generates income through rent and appreciates over time, offering a stable and permissible way to build wealth.

Key Strategy: Shariah-Compliant Investment Funds

Shariah-compliant mutual funds or ETFs allow Muslims to diversify their investments across various industries, ensuring that their portfolio is both profitable and halal. These funds screen companies for compliance with Islamic principles, avoiding industries like alcohol, gambling, or interest-based finance.

5. Integrity in Business and Financial Dealings

Integrity is a fundamental aspect of Islamic teachings, especially in financial dealings. Muslims are required to be honest and transparent in all business transactions, ensuring that all parties involved are treated fairly and equitably.

Key Principle: Transparency and Fairness

Islamic finance emphasizes **fairness** in all contracts, ensuring that neither party is exploited. Contracts must be clear, with all terms agreed upon upfront to avoid disputes or misunderstandings.

Hadith Reference:

The Prophet Muhammad (PBUH) said: *"The seller and the buyer have the right to keep or return goods as long as they have not parted, and if they spoke the truth and made clear the defects, then they would be blessed in their bargain."* (Sahih al-Bukhari)

6. Leaving a Legacy Through Ethical Wealth Distribution

Wealth in Islam is seen as a **means** to fulfill both individual needs and societal obligations. Ensuring that wealth is distributed ethically, both during one's life and after death, is crucial.

Key Strategy: Islamic Inheritance Law

Islam provides clear guidelines for inheritance to ensure that wealth is distributed fairly among heirs. Following these guidelines ensures that wealth is not concentrated in the hands of a few and that all family members receive their rightful share.

Key Strategy: Endowments (Waqf)

A **Waqf** is an Islamic endowment, typically set up to fund charitable causes such as education, healthcare, or religious institutions. By establishing a Waqf, Muslims can leave a lasting legacy that benefits society long after their death.

Key Verse:

"Indeed, the men who practice charity and the women who practice charity and [they who] have loaned Allah a goodly loan - it will be multiplied for them, and they will have a noble reward."
(Surah Al-Hadid 57:18)

Conclusion: Wealth as a Means to Serve Allah and Society

Building long-term wealth with integrity in Islam involves adhering to principles of fairness, transparency, and social responsibility. By avoiding haram investments, engaging in ethical business practices, and contributing to the welfare of society through Zakat and charity, Muslims can ensure that their wealth-building efforts are both sustainable and aligned with Islamic values. Ultimately, wealth in Islam is a tool for achieving not just personal prosperity but also the greater good, ensuring that one's financial success benefits others and earns the blessings of Allah.

Case Studies of Successful Muslim Investors

Case Studies of Successful Muslim Investors

Islamic finance has gained global recognition, and many successful Muslim investors have navigated the world of finance while adhering to Islamic principles. These individuals have applied Shariah-compliant strategies to build wealth in industries like technology, real estate, and entrepreneurship. Here are real-world examples of Muslim investors who have achieved financial success while staying true to their faith.

1. Sheikh Saleh Kamel – Pioneering Islamic Finance

Sheikh **Saleh Kamel** was one of the pioneers of modern Islamic finance and an influential Saudi businessman. As the founder of **Dallah Al-Baraka Group**, a multinational conglomerate with interests in banking, real estate, and media, Sheikh Kamel was instrumental in establishing some of the first Islamic financial institutions, including **Al Baraka Banking Group**.

Key Contributions :

- Sheikh Kamel established **Islamic banks** in the 1970s, offering riba-free financial products to the Muslim community.
- His ventures in Islamic finance focused on ethical investments in sectors like healthcare, media, and infrastructure, ensuring that they complied with Shariah law.
- His work helped globalize Islamic banking, making it a trusted and accessible option for Muslims around the world.

Success Insight : Sheikh Kamel's success stemmed from his dedication to creating financial products that aligned with Islamic principles, promoting transparency, fairness, and shared risk. His legacy lives on through the vast network of Islamic financial institutions that operate globally today.

2. Prince Al-Waleed bin Talal – Ethical Real Estate and Technology Investments

Prince Al-Waleed bin Talal is a Saudi billionaire and one of the most prominent Muslim investors globally. He is the founder of **Kingdom Holding Company**, which has investments in real estate, hospitality, and technology. Al-Waleed's approach to investing is rooted in Islamic principles, especially when it comes to ethical investments.

Key Investments :

- Al-Waleed invested in **Islamic-compliant real estate**, including the development of iconic projects like the **Kingdom Tower** in Riyadh.
- He is also known for his **Shariah-compliant technology investments**, including stakes in companies like **Apple**, **Twitter**, and **Citigroup**, where he ensured that his investments avoided interest-based earnings.

Success Insight : Prince Al-Waleed's strategy involves investing in diverse sectors while adhering to Islamic values. He ensures that his wealth is invested in ethical ventures, contributing to the well-being of society. His disciplined approach to managing wealth within Islamic frameworks has made him one of the most successful Muslim investors globally.

3. Iqbal Khan – Innovator in Islamic Finance

Iqbal Khan is a prominent figure in Islamic finance, credited with developing Shariah-compliant financial products for Muslim investors. He played a pivotal role in establishing **HSBC Amanah**, the Islamic banking arm of HSBC, which offers Shariah-compliant financial products globally.

Key Contributions :

- Iqbal Khan pioneered the introduction of **Islamic bonds (Sukuk)**, allowing Muslim investors to engage in debt markets without violating the prohibition of *riba*.

- He also developed **Islamic mutual funds** and **Shariah-compliant private equity**, giving Muslim investors access to diversified financial instruments.

Success Insight : Iqbal Khan's success came from his ability to innovate within the boundaries of Islamic law, creating financial tools that allowed Muslims to participate in the global financial market while upholding their religious obligations. His work opened new avenues for ethical investing in Islamic finance.

4. Azmi Mikati – Telecommunications and Shariah-Compliant Investments

Azmi Mikati, a Lebanese businessman, is the CEO of **M1 Group**, a multinational investment holding company. M1 Group operates across diverse sectors, including telecommunications, real estate, and aviation. Mikati has successfully maintained Shariah-compliant practices in his business dealings, especially in the telecommunications industry.

Key Achievements :

- Under Mikati's leadership, M1 Group expanded its operations globally while adhering to ethical business practices, ensuring transparency and fairness in all financial dealings.

- His investments focus on **socially responsible projects** that align with Islamic values, such as infrastructure development in underserved regions.

Success Insight : Azmi Mikati's adherence to ethical business practices, even in highly competitive industries, has positioned him as a leader in the telecommunications world.

His success demonstrates that Shariah-compliant investing is not only possible but also highly profitable when approached with discipline and integrity.

5. Dr. Mohamed A. El-Erian – Ethical Investing in Global Markets

Dr. Mohamed A. El-Erian is a prominent Muslim economist and former CEO of **PIMCO**, one of the world's largest investment management firms. Though his career spans conventional finance, Dr. El-Erian's investment philosophy is deeply rooted in ethical principles and social responsibility, reflecting Islamic values in finance.

Key Contributions :

- Dr. El-Erian has been a vocal advocate of **sustainable and ethical investing**, emphasizing the importance of balancing profits with social responsibility.
- He has highlighted the role of **ethical finance** in promoting long-term stability, advising investors to consider both financial returns and their social impact.

Success Insight : Dr. El-Erian's approach to investing aligns with Islamic finance principles by emphasizing the importance of ethical decision-making in financial markets. His success in global finance demonstrates the viability of integrating Shariah principles with modern investment strategies.

Conclusion: Learning from Success

These case studies of successful Muslim investors show how adherence to Islamic principles in finance can lead to significant success. By focusing on ethical investing, avoiding *riba* (interest), and ensuring transparency and fairness, these individuals have made substantial contributions to both their personal wealth and the broader community. Their journeys offer valuable insights for Muslims looking to navigate the world of Islamic finance while staying true to their faith.

Conclusion: A Path to Ethical Wealth

A Path to Ethical Wealth

This book has explored the principles and practices of wealth management in Islam, focusing on building, preserving, and distributing wealth in a manner that is both ethical and sustainable. From avoiding *riba* (interest) and engaging in Shariah-compliant investments, to fulfilling obligations like **Zakat** and maintaining financial discipline, the essence of Islamic wealth management revolves around the idea that wealth is a blessing from Allah and must be handled with responsibility, integrity, and fairness.

Key Takeaways

1. Wealth as a Blessing and a Responsibility

Wealth is a gift from Allah, but it is also a test. Muslims are reminded to view their wealth not only as a means of personal enjoyment but as an opportunity to help others and contribute to the broader well-being of society. This perspective transforms wealth from a purely material pursuit into a spiritual responsibility.

- **Verse Reminder**:
  "But seek, through that which Allah has given you, the home of the Hereafter; and [yet], do not forget your share of the world." (Surah Al-Qasas 28:77)

This verse reflects the balance Islam encourages between using wealth for worldly needs while also investing in the Hereafter through charitable deeds, responsible spending, and ethical investing.

2. Avoiding Riba and Engaging in Halal Financial Practices

A central theme of this book has been the prohibition of *riba* (interest). The importance of avoiding interest-based transactions cannot be overstated in Islam. Instead, Muslims are encouraged to seek out halal alternatives, such as **Murabaha** (cost-plus financing), **Ijara** (leasing), and **Mudarabah** (profit-sharing).

By engaging in Shariah-compliant financial transactions, Muslims ensure that their wealth is earned and grown in ways that are aligned with their faith. Islamic finance promotes fairness, transparency, and mutual benefit, protecting both the lender and borrower from exploitation.

3. Ethical Investing and Wealth Distribution

The book emphasized the importance of investing in halal industries that align with Islamic values, such as ethical technology, sustainable agriculture, and socially responsible businesses. Ethical investing allows Muslims to build wealth while ensuring that their financial activities contribute positively to society.

Moreover, **Zakat** (obligatory charity) plays a vital role in redistributing wealth, reducing inequality, and supporting the less fortunate. By fulfilling their Zakat obligations, Muslims purify their wealth and help uplift those in need, reinforcing the community-oriented approach to wealth in Islam.

The Benefits of Adhering to Ethical Principles

Adhering to Islamic ethical principles in wealth management brings numerous benefits:

1. **Spiritual Fulfillment** : Wealth accumulated and managed in compliance with Shariah brings blessings and spiritual growth. It reinforces the Muslim's relationship with Allah and ensures that wealth becomes a source of spiritual elevation rather than moral decay.

2. **Sustainable Wealth Growth** : By investing in long-term, sustainable sectors like real estate, halal mutual funds, and ethical industries, Muslims can build wealth steadily and securely, avoiding the high-risk and speculative practices prohibited in Islam.

3. **Social Responsibility** : Islamic wealth management encourages contributions to the well-being of society through charity, ethical investments, and responsible business practices. This not only benefits the individual but helps build a more just and equitable society.

4. **Financial Integrity** : Islamic finance promotes fairness, transparency, and accountability in all transactions. Whether through profit-sharing models like **Mudarabah** or ethical investments in halal sectors, Muslims can maintain financial integrity while pursuing wealth.

A Call to Action: Living the Path of Ethical Wealth

In conclusion, Islamic wealth management is not just a set of rules for growing and managing money—it is a holistic approach to living in accordance with Allah's guidance. By adhering to these principles, Muslims can achieve both material success and spiritual fulfilment. Wealth becomes a means to serve Allah, uplift others, and contribute to the betterment of society.

Wealth built with integrity brings lasting benefits, not only in this world but also in the Hereafter. Muslims are called to live by these principles, ensuring that their pursuit of wealth reflects the values of justice, fairness, and compassion that are central to Islam.

May your path to building ethical wealth be blessed with success, peace, and fulfillment, both in this world and the Hereafter.

www.ingramcontent.com/pod-product-compliance
Lightning Source LLC
Chambersburg PA
CBHW070411230526
45471CB00006B/2746